easy INDian vegetarian cookery

by
Ashra Kumari Burman

Published by INSAAF Communications

Milton Keynes, Buckinghamshire.

Email: Insaaf77@sky.com

Cataloguing-in-Publication Data
A catalogue record for this book is available from the British Library.

ISBN 978-0-9561088-0-7

Printed and bound in the United Kingdom by Swan Print Ltd., Bedford.
Special edition: In memory of my youngest brother Ashan Kumar
'Seany' Burman (1966-2007).

Thank you to Stuart for the design and typesetting of this book.

Front cover and illustrations by Achar Kumar Burman.

ॐ: CONTENTS

Shanti ♥ Shakti

Peace   Love   Strength

❧:INTRODUCTION

Outside India, Indian cooking is often just known as one word "Curry." This term very loosely describes a typical Indian dish. The word originates from 'Khari' – an Indian cooking pot, and is a corruption of the Tamil word "kari" which means "sauce." However, the following recipes are not simply about "making a curry"- they are about making Indian food, which have their own special names, spices and tastes. The recipes and methods in this book are based upon the traditional cooking techniques of Punjabi people who live in the north-western province of India, which was where I was born.

"Sabji" (pronounced subjee)is the name given to the various spiced Vegetable dishes. Sabji can either be "Sukha" which means "dry", so there is not much liquid in the dish, or "Durri" which is a thinner watery spicy sauce. The recipes are not very chilli "hot" as I feel this ruins the taste of the essential spices. It also enables children to participate in the enjoyment of eating.

I have included Dhal which is a dish made out of beans or pulses; as well as the popular triangular shaped Samosa and Onion fritters commonly known as Pakora & Onion Bhajis.

Indian breads are known as Roti or Chapati, Paratha and Poori. With a little practice, I know you will be able to become quite an expert in making all of these delicious breads!

❧:INTRODUCTION

I have included only one Rice dish, which happens to be my favourite. I have purposely kept to a few recipes, so as to keep the book simple and basic.

I hope, therefore, that my introduction will lead you to try many other sophisticated tastes of Indian food - as Indian cooking is a rich story of geography, religion & beliefs!

TRIBUTE

Being the eldest and being a daughter of a traditional Hindu-Punjabi family, I was taught how to cook Indian food at a very early age; not only by my Mother, but also by my Father (there's a drawing of him at the beginning of the book cutting an Onion). They taught me with such tenderness and great patience that I owe all my skill and knowledge of Indian food to them.

I must mention Neil, Linda and my son Paulie, who I know are proud of my efforts at writing. Thanks to Brenda for proof-reading. And finally to my brother Achar Kumar 'Billy' Burman for his beautiful illustrations.

2

ॐ : VEGETARIANISM AND VEGANISM

I have been a Vegetarian for over 20 years and Vegan for the past 15 years. The recipes in this book are suitable for both Vegetarians and Vegans.

I would like to share the sentiments echoed in an ancient Chinese verse that vividly describes the bad karma generated by the killing of animals.

"For hundreds of thousands of years
    the stew in the pot
has brewed hatred and resentment
    that is difficult to stop.
If you wish to know why there are disasters of
    armies and weapons in the world,
    listen to the piteous cries
From the slaughterhouse at midnight."

Taken from "A Buddhist Case for Vegetarianism" by R. P. Kapleau.

Spices should be stored in airtight containers out of the light.

GARAM MASALA

A mixture of various spices; usually Cumin Seeds, Cloves, Cinnamon, Cardamons and Bay Leaves.

ADRAK

Ginger (fresh root or ground).
This pungent root aids digestion and is a good source of zinc.

DHANIA

Coriander. Gives subtle fragrance.

MIRCH

I tend to use the thin long green chillies. High source of Vitamin C & strengthens the immune system.

JEERA

Cumin (seeds and ground powder).

ஐ :VARIOUS INDIAN SPICES USED

Try grinding your own rather than relying on the packets.
You'll find that the spices become infinitely more aromatic.

LASSON

Garlic (fresh is best). Rich in Potassium
& nature's most effective antibiotic.

HALDI

Turmeric (saffron yellow). A wonder
spice as it helps to detoxify the
liver, balance cholestrol, enhances the
complexion & improves circulation.

ANARDANA

Dried Pomegranate seeds.
Fights skin ageing.

DAL CHEENEE

Cinnamon sticks. Beneficial for colds &
sore throats; it also aids digestion.

CHAT MASALA

Blend of Black salt, Chilli powder, Cumin
seeds and dry tangy Mango Powder.

OILS

"Ghee" is the traditional cooking medium of India. I tend to use either Sunflower or Olive Oil when cooking. I prefer using Sea Salt, as its so rich in minerals and brings out the flavour of the spices.

FLOUR AND EQUIPMENT

The flour I use for making Indian breads is known as "Atta" or Chapati flour. It comes in various grades and is a wholegrain flour which can be bought in Indian stores and some supermarkets.

Tava

This is an Indian flat pan/griddle. It is slightly concave in the centre which is what helps to cook the breads evenly. It's not very expensive to buy from Indian stores or on-line. A real must if you want to make lots of Indian breads.

KARAHI

This is similar to a Chinese Wok, but much heavier. It is ideal for deep frying things such as Poori, Samosa and Pakora. The best alternative to a Karahi is a deep fat frying pan.

1: INDIAN BREADS

 ## ROTI/CHAPATI

It is a Wholewheat, light griddle bread. It is the best known
Indian bread and is a thin, unleavened cooked dough that puffs up
during the last stage of cooking. I tend to use the word Roti.

INGREDIENTS:

450grams/16oz of Atta Flour
237ml/8oz of warm water
Small bowl of dry Atta flour for dusting and rolling out the Roti
Tava or a shallow frying pan

Makes about 5 Roti.

METHOD:

1. Put the flour into a large bowl, make a well and add the water a little
   at a time to form a dough and firmly knead it.

2. Cover and leave to rest for 15-30 minutes - in the fridge is best if
   you really want good results.

3. When ready to cook, gently heat the Tava.

4. Break off a small piece of dough, around 6.5cm/2½" and shape
   it into a round ball. Do this by putting the dough onto the palm
   of one hand and using the fingers of the other hand fold the edges
   tightly into the centre of the ball, then smooth it in the palm of
   your hand into a ball. Best to roll out five balls now, so that you
   know you have divided the dough up equally.

5. Dip and dust this ball into a little dry flour to prevent it from sticking to the rolling surface and then roll it out into a thin round no more than 3mm thick and about 16.5cm/6½" in diameter. Use more dry flour if you find the dough keeps sticking to the surface. Remember though before placing the Roti onto the Tava, to flick off any surplus flour. This is very important, otherwise it will not cook evenly. This can be done by quickly passing the Roti from one palm of the hand to the other.

6. To test whether the Tava is hot enough, place a tiny bit of dough onto it and if it burns too quickly, reduce the heat. With a little practice you will be able to assess the right temperature.

7. Carefully place the rolled-out Roti onto the hot Tava. As soon as the top side becomes transparent, which should only take about five seconds, turn the Roti over and cook until small bubbles appear. Then turn it over again onto its original side and with kitchen paper or a clean tea towel or your fingers carefully press the Roti all over, this will make it magically rise and puff up. You may need to turn and cook both sides once more for just a couple of seconds, and as soon as the Roti has light golden brown patches on both sides it is cooked. Another method to make the Roti rise is to place the original cooked side underneath a hot grill.

8. Remove the Roti from the Tava and smear with a little sunflower oil or Ghee (this is optional). Best served at once.

1: INDIAN BREADS

To eat Roti simply tear off a small piece of the bread and scoop up some of the Dhal or Sabji, then pop the whole parcel into your mouth! You can also make Roti wraps by rolling your favourite Sabji onto the cooked Roti and rolling it into a pancake roll.

 ## POORI

Crispy wholewheat deep fried bread – kids just love eating these!

+ 340g/12oz of Atta flour
+ 150ml/5floz of warm water
+ 2 tablespoons of Oil in a small bowl
+ 2 litres (3½ pints) of oil for frying

Makes about 10 Pooris

METHOD:

1. Place the flour in a bowl and pour a little water at a time to bind the flour into quite a stiffish dough, a little stiffer than you would make for Rotis. Cover and leave to stand for 10 minutes in the fridge.

2. Break off a small piece of the dough about 4cm (1½") round ball. And do this until you have 10 balls ready to roll out.

3. Gently heat the oil in a large pan. To find out whether it is hot enough, drop a small piece of the dough into it. If it starts sizzling immediately and floats to the top, then the oil is just right.

4. Dip one side of the ball into the small bowl of cold oil and start rolling the dough into a round of no more than 12cm (5") in diameter and as thin as you can get it. (No dry flour is needed for making Poori).

Note: Getting the Oil in the pan to the right temperature is very important, otherwise the Poori will not puff up. The hotter the oil the better, however, do be careful not to burn the oil.

5. Lift the rolled Poori which will be oily and sticky carefully off the surface and slip it into the hot oil.

6. Immediately using a perforated ladle gently keep pressing and slightly twisting the Poori in the oil for just 2 minutes. The Poori should rise, when it does, quickly turn it over and do the same to the other side. This time the Poori should puff up like a balloon. Leave it to fry for literally two seconds more on both sides until very light golden brown. (If it doesn't rise it usually means that the oil is not hot enough).

7. Lift the Poori out of the oil with the ladle and hold it at an angle against the side of the pan for a few seconds so as to drain away any excess oil.

A Poori is best eaten straight away with a Sabji or Dhal. Although as a child I often ate them cold at picnics and they still tasted really good!

1: INDIAN BREADS

PARATHAS

These are plain or stuffed shallow fried bread. They can be eaten hot or cold and are ideal for picnics and freeze really well. The recipe below is for Parathas stuffed with Potatoes and Onion.

STUFFED ONION & POTATO PARATHA

INGREDIENTS:

- 450g/16oz Atta flour
- 250ml/½ pint tepid water
- 4 tablespoons Oil in a bowl, or 4 tablespoons of Ghee
- Little bowl of dry Atta flour
- 2 tablespoons of Atta flour for making the Paste

FILLING:

This can be either chopped Onion, grated Cauliflower; cooked mashed Lentils, or left-overs from a dry Sabji. For this recipe I've used mashed Potato with diced Onion.

- 3 medium sized Potatoes, peeled and cut into quarters
- ½ medium sized Onion, chopped very finely
- 2 heaped teaspoons of Garam Masala
- ½ level teaspoon of Chilli powder (or one finely chopped fresh green Chilli)
- 1 teaspoon of dried Pomegranate seeds (optional)
- 1 level teaspoon Salt

Makes 3 stuffed Parathas.

1: INDIAN BREADS

There are two ways of making stuffed Parathas - choose the one that suits you.

METHOD ONE FOR MAKING STUFFED PARATHAS:

1. Use the same process for making the dough as you did for making Roti. (See page 7).

2. Make 6 even dough balls of 5cm/2" in diameter.

3. Then prepare the filling. Boil the peeled Potatoes (not too soft) and mash. Finely dice the Onion and mix them into the mashed Potato.

4. Add all the spices next in any order to the Potato and Onion mixture and mix together – leave to cool down.

5. Make the paste by putting 2 tablespoons of Atta flour in a little bowl and mix with a little cold water until you get a soft paste, rather like glue.

6. Roll out two small Roti rounds, 16.5cm/6½" in diameter. These will be used to make one stuffed Paratha. You may need to use a little dry flour under the rounds so that they are not sticking to the surface.

7. Spread some of the oil thinly to the surface of both rounds and right to the edge of the rounds. Put 3 heaped tablespoons of the filling onto one round and spread it evenly.

8. Put a little paste around the edges of both rounds.

9. Place the other rolled out round on top of this as if to make a sandwich. Very gently press down the edges.

10. Carefully roll the stuffed Paratha out into a slightly larger round, no more than 20.5cm/8" using just a little dry flour if it is sticking to the surface.

11. Heat up the Tava to a fairly high temperature and carefully place the stuffed Paratha onto it. Reduce the heat a little.

12. Allow this to cook for about two minutes, then carefully turn the Paratha over. Spread some oil (approximately two teaspoons) and use the back of the same teaspoon to spread the oil evenly on this slightly cooked side and allow the underneath side to cook for a minute or so. Then turn the Paratha over, smear the same amount of oil on this side, so that you now have oil smeared on both sides, as well as both sides being slightly cooked.

13. Turn the Paratha over once more until both sides are crisp and golden. (Again you may have to raise or lower the heat from time to time and if it is not quite cooked you may have to turn it over again and cook both sides for another minute).

14. Remove the Paratha carefully from the Tava otherwise the filling may fall out.

Stuffed Paratha is usually eaten with Indian pickles, and/or with Natural Plain or Soya Yoghurt.

METHOD TWO FOR MAKING STUFFED PARATHAS:

I found when teaching my son (who by the way cooks inspiring dishes), how to make stuffed Parathas - he preferred this method. So I'll share it with you.

Using the same ingredients for the first method of making Parathas - this time though make a much bigger ball of Roti dough 7.5cm/3" and roll it out to 12.5cm/5" round.

Take 2 heaped tablespoons of the cooled down filling mixture of Potatoes and Onions and place in the middle of the round. Now pull in all sides of the dough tightly into the centre of the round, until the dough covers all the filling. Flatten the round out a little with your hand before starting to roll it out.

Very carefully, using a slight a bit of dry Atta flour, roll it out into 20.5cm/8" – you'll find that the creases in the pastry will miraculously disappear after the rolling. Now cook it the same way as you would for the first method of making Parathas, turning it over and spreading the oil on both sides etc. By using this second method, the stuffed Paratha looks neat, quicker to make; needs no paste and the filling definitely does not fall out!

1: INDIAN BREADS

 ## PLAIN PARATHA

This is a layered flaky flat bread.

This method makes about five Plain Parathas. It makes a change from Chapati and is great for freezing. Use the same ingredients outlined for making Stuffed Parathas. (See page 11).

METHOD:

1. Make the dough, using the same quantity and method you did for the Roti, which is 450grams/16oz Atta Flour.
   You will also need a small bowl of dry flour and a small bowl of oil 150ml/5fl.oz. Using Ghee also works well.

2. Shape the dough into a 5cm/2" balls.

3. Flatten one of the balls and roll into a very small round 10cm/4". Brush it liberally with oil or Ghee. Fold the sides inwards to the middle of the round to make a square shape, making sure the sides overlap each other, so as to make a square parcel. Roll this out to a slightly bigger square shape with all sides measuring approx 15.5cm/6". Use some dry flour to help you, but remember to get rid of the excess flour before placing it onto the Tava.

4. Heat the Tava to quite a high temperature and place the Plain Paratha onto it. Cook it for half a minute then turn it over. Spread some oil on this slightly cooked side, (I use a teaspoon), and repeat the process for the other side – it's a similar method to making stuffed Parathas. When both sides are crisp and golden brown it is cooked.

1: INDIAN BREADS

Plain Paratha can be eaten with a Sabji or simply with some Indian pickles as a little snack. I think they are such an interesting shape; simply delicious and very quick to make. Try spreading honey or maple syrup on them for breakfast. Simply delicious sweet version!

2: SNACKS

SAMOSA

These are deep-fried stuffed vegetable savoury pasties in a triangular shape. They do take a long time to prepare but they are worth the time and effort. Get a friend or the family to help!

PASTRY

- 340g/12oz Plain White or Plain Wholemeal Flour – not Atta flour.
- 250ml/½ pint of cold water
- 2 tablespoons of the same flour to be used for making the Paste

METHOD FOR MAKING THE PASTRY:

1. Put the flour into a bowl and make a well in the middle; add the water a little at a time to make a stiff dough.

2. Cover the dough and set aside while you prepare the filling.

Note: You will need to make some paste to help stick down all the edges of the pastry to make the triangular shape. After making the pastry mix two tablespoons of flour with a little water until you get a soft paste forming, rather like glue.

FILLING:

- 3 medium sized Potatoes
- 2 tablespoons Oil for frying the onion
- 1 small Onion, finely chopped
- 225g/8oz Garden Peas (fresh or frozen)
- 1 teaspoon Salt
- 1 teaspoon of Chilli Powder or 1 fresh green Chilli finely chopped
- 2 heaped teaspoons of Garam Masala
- 1 heaped tablespoons of coarsely chopped fresh Coriander leaves. (optional)
- 2 litres of oil for deep frying

2: SNACKS

Makes about 16 Samosas.

TO PREPARE FILLING:

1. Boil the Potatoes, let them cool and peel. (I always boil Potatoes with their skins on and peel them once boiled, as I believe this retains more of the goodness of the Potato skin.) Mash the Potatoes. Then peel and dice the Onion.

2. In a small pan, heat up two tablespoons Oil and fry the Onion until it is a light golden brown and add the Garam Masala, Chilli, and Salt. Then mix in the mashed Potato and lastly the slightly cooked frozen Peas. (If you are using fresh Peas, then you will have to boil them first until soft). Stir fry for about a minute. Taste to see if you need more Salt or Chilli powder.

3. Allow the Samosa filling to cool and add the freshly chopped Coriander leaves.

SHAPING THE PASTRY:

1. Make 8 balls of 5cm/2" in size. Roll one out very thinly (the thinner you can get the better), into a small pancake size, using a very little amount of flour to just help you roll out the round of no more than 16.5cm/6½" in diameter.

Note: If you want the pastry to be quite crispy you will now need to bake the round on the Tava or a shallow frying pan for just half a minute both sides, so that it is warmed up and not cooked through. You can use filo pastry to make them even crispier!

①

②

③ ← Paste edges ...

④

⑤ fold both sides into centre to form a seam...

⑥

⑦ turn cone around...

⑧ fill with more filling, if space...

⑨ ⌐ Press top edge together...

⑩ check all seams are secure, if not, add more paste ..

KETCHUP 100% OK

MANO MANARS ACHAR MIXX & PICKLE PACHRANGA

2. Cut the small round of pastry in half and put one heaped teaspoon of the mixture in the centre of the semi circle. Now smear some of the paste you made earlier around all the edges of the pastry.

3. To fold the semi-circle pastry to get it into the triangular shape, place the semi circle with the (straight edge), at the top on your surface **(see diagram on page 19)**. Now fold the left side of the pastry towards the centre over the stuffing - then fold the right side of the pastry also towards the centre just over the seam of the left side to make a cone shape. Still holding up the cone in your left hand, seal the centre together by pressing it gently, making sure the tip of the cone has no gap at all otherwise the stuffing will fall out the bottom and it will not cook through. Holding up the cone, open the top part and insert another teaspoon of the stuffing, then simply press together the top part of the cone to seal it - you now have the triangular shape! *It is best to deep fry two or three Samosas as soon as you have folded them as they start sticking to the surface.*

4. Heat the oil to quite a fairly hot temperature. Carefully lower as many Samosas into the hot oil as you can to fit into the pan, making sure that they don't clash with each other, otherwise they may come apart in the oil. Fry for about three minutes until golden brown, turning them over very gently. You will need to reduce the heat now to cook the next batch - it is a case of regulating the oil. Toss the Samosa onto absorbent kitchen paper to get rid of the excess oil. Serve with Tomato ketchup and/or Indian pickles.

2: SNACKS

 ## PAKORA & ONION BHAJIS

Pakora is a crispy, deep fried vegetable in special batter and is usually served as a snack in India, particularly for guests. Chopped uncooked vegetables such as Cauliflower, Aubergine, or a mixture of Spinach, Onion and Potato works really well. The batter is made with the flour of split black Chick Peas known as BASEN or GRAM flour. The recipe and method for making Pakora and Onion Bhajis is the same.
For this recipe I am keeping it simple using Onions and Coriander. Makes about 14 pieces. Serve with Tomato, Brown or Chilli Sauce, or mix all three together for a tasty sauce.

INGREDIENTS:

- 280g/10oz GRAM flour
- 1½ level teaspoons of Salt
- 2 heaped teaspoons of Cumin seeds
- 1 heaped teaspoon of Chilli powder
- 1 heaped teaspoon of Garam Masala
- 1 heaped teaspoon of Turmeric
- 8 stems of Coriander leaves – discard the stems or 1 heaped teaspoon of Coriander powder
- 2 medium sized Onions cut in half, very thinly sliced lengthways to form long strips
- 325ml/11floz of cold water
- 2 litres of oil for deep frying in a large pan

METHOD:

1. Cut the Onion in half first, then slice into long strips and put to one side.

2. Put the Gram flour into a large bowl add and mix the spices, oil, salt and coriander

3. Make a well in the middle and add the water a little at a time, mixing the batter really thoroughly and as smooth as you can get it. Add the Onions, making sure they are well coated with the batter.

4. Put the batter aside for five minutes to settle while you heat up the oil in a deep fat frying pan. (To test whether the oil is hot enough, drop a tiny bit of the batter and when it rises to the top sizzling, the oil is ready.)

5. Scoop up a big tablespoon of the batter and drop this gently into the hot oil using another tablespoon to help you guide it in. Fry for a minute and take out any crinkly bits. Use a perforated ladle to turn them over and fry for another 3 minutes until they become a very deep golden brown. Once the first batch has been cooked, best to now turn the heat down, otherwise the hot oil can easily burn the Onion Bhajis and they will not be cooked through. You may have to keep regulating the heat of the oil.

6. Drain the Onion Bhajis onto absorbent kitchen paper. They cook into really interesting spikey shapes and are great messy fun food to make!

Note: When using Aubergines, cut into finely sliced wedges or strips, leaving the skin on. Aubergine cooks much quicker, so be careful not to burn them. If using Cauliflower, cut them into very small florets. Spinach is also best thinly sliced and you can add finely sliced Onion as well as tiny cubed Potatoes with Spinach to make Pakoras. In fact try combinations of various vegetables that you prefer and give it a go. Experiment by adding more of the spices to suit your own taste.

3: SABJI

"Sabji" is the name given to any Vegetable that has been cooked with a variety of Indian spices. The "Masala" (which means a mixture of spices), is used as a basis for making a Sabji. Different spices are used to suit a particular type of Vegetable and different approaches are used to enhance the flavour of the particular Vegetable.

I have chosen to use the following vegetables and chickpeas for making a sukha sabji:

Aloo Gobhi – spicy Potatoes and Cauliflower
Aloo Baingan – spicy Potatoes and Aubergine
Bhindi – spicy fried Okra
Channa Masala – spicy chick peas in a rich tomato sauce

 ## ALOO GOBHI
Spicy Potatoes and Cauliflower dish

INGREDIENTS:

+ 1 medium sized cauliflower
+ 3 medium sized potatoes
+ 3 medium sized onions – finely chopped

3: SABJI

MASALA INGREDIENTS:

+ 4 cloves Garlic – crushed or finely chopped
+ 2.5cm long and 1cm width (1" long & half an inch wide)
  of Fresh Ginger or 1 level teaspoon of Dried Ginger powder
+ 2 fresh thin green chillies – finely chopped or ½ level teaspoon
  of Chilli powder
+ 2 heaped teaspoons of Garam Masala powder
+ 2 heaped teaspoons of Haldi (Turmeric) powder
+ 1 level teaspoon of Salt
+ 1 heaped tablespoon of chopped fresh Coriander leaves
+ 6 tablespoons of oil
+ 170ml/6floz of cold water
+ A large saucepan with lid

Serves 6 people

METHOD:

1. Cut the Cauliflower into medium-sized florets discarding
   the green leaves, (although my Mum used to chop these up
   and add them too!). Wash the pieces and leave to drain.

2. Next peel the Potatoes, and cut into 4cm/1½" diameter and
   into 2.5cm/1" chunks. I tend to cut the potatoes lengthways
   first as I find it easier to get the desired chunks.

3. Scrape the peel off the fresh Ginger and chop it finely.
   Peel and finely chop the Garlic and Onions.

24

4. Heat the Oil and add the Onions, Garlic, Ginger and the fresh Chillies at this stage. Fry until golden brown, stirring to make sure it doesn't stick to the pan.

5. Add the spices in the following order: Turmeric, Garam Masala, Chilli Power (if not using fresh Chillies) and Salt. Mix the spices all together for a few seconds.

6. Now add the Potatoes and 170ml/6fl.oz of water and simmer on a low heat, with the saucepan lid on for about half an hour as the Potatoes take much longer to cook than the Cauliflower. You will need to stir the Potatoes every 5 to 10 minutes as it is important that the sauce does not stick to the bottom of the pan. After 10 minutes, add a little more water, around 114ml/4fl.oz. You will need to allow approx 20 minutes for the Potatoes to be almost cooked. After 20 minutes, add the Cauliflower pieces and mix these to the rich sauce and simmer on a low heat. Again you will need to check this dish every 5 to 10 minutes as it will need a gentle stir each time you check it. It will take about 15 minutes to cook the Cauliflower.

7. Check if the Potatoes are soft and if they are, the dish is ready. Finally sprinkle fresh Coriander leaves on top.

Aloo Gobhi is best eaten with Roti or with plain Basmati Rice, or even as a filling for Pitta bread and if in a hurry use it as a filling for Sandwiches!

3: SABJI

 ## ALOO BAINGAN SABJI

Potato & Aubergine dish

INGREDIENTS:

- 2 medium sized Aubergines
- 3 medium sized Potatoes
- 3 medium sized Onions
- 3 fresh Tomatoes finely chopped or a small tin of tomatoes (225g)

METHOD:

Use the same spices and method as for ALOO GOBHI and again add the Potatoes first and allow them to cook for half an hour on a medium heat - then add the Aubergine, making sure that all the sauce covers it. Best to cut off the stem of the Aubergine and I tend to cut the Aubergine lengthways first then slice into the half round shapes of approx 2.5cm/1".

Serves 6 people

This dish cooks in about 20 minutes.

3: SABJI

STUFFED AUBERGINE

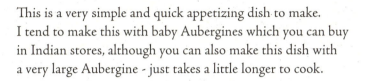

·AUBERGINES·

with Chunky Red Onions

This is a very simple and quick appetizing dish to make.
I tend to make this with baby Aubergines which you can buy
in Indian stores, although you can also make this dish with
a very large Aubergine - just takes a little longer to cook.

INGREDIENTS:

- 1 really large Aubergine OR use 6 baby Aubergines
- 3 medium Red Onions (although White Onions will do)
- 6 stems of Coriander leaves (keep the leaves – discard the stems)

SPICY AUBERGINE PASTE - for this you will need:

- 2 heaped teaspoons of Garam Masala
- 2 heaped teaspoons of Turmeric
- 1 level teaspoon of Chilli powder
- 1 level teaspoon of Salt
- 1 heaped tablespoon of Chat Masala powder (optional)
- 6 tablespoons of Oil (I prefer to use Olive Oil for the paste)
- Sunflower Oil to fry

Serves 4 people

METHOD:

Mix all the spicy Aubergine paste into 4 tablespoons of Oil.

Keep the stem of the Aubergine on and the same when using
baby Aubergines as this helps to keep the Aubergine/s in tact for
stuffing and frying.

3: SABJI

If using a large Aubergine it is important to slice it downwards from the tip end to the stem, into four long quarters making sure you stop cutting just before the stem. It should open up like a flower if you hold the stem at the bottom. Now put the Aubergine under a hot grill for five minutes, turning it over to just soften the skin, not to cook it. Do the same if using baby Aubergines, cutting them into four long slices down towards the stem and bake under the grill until slightly soft.

Take the spicy Aubergine paste and smear this liberally with a spoon on all sides of the slices, covering as much of the white flesh of the Aubergine/s.

Put some Oil into a large frying pan and add the Aubergine/s and fry on a gentle heat making sure that all the sides have been cooked. This can take up to 15 minutes and a little longer if its a big Aubergine.

NOTE: *Halfway through the cooking of the Aubergine/s add the roughly chopped onions to one side of the pan, and add a little more oil – and you'll find that the juices from the Aubergine will seep into the Onions which will make them taste quite sensational.*

I think this dish makes you look like a real professional cook – yet is so easy to make, hence the title of this book!

I usually serve the Aubergine/s on a plate of plain cooked Basmati Rice and decorate it with some freshly chopped Coriander leaves, as well as a sprinkling of the irresistible Chat Masala.

3: SABJI

 ## BHINDI SABJI – Okra

INGREDIENTS:

- Quarter kilo 0.25kg/9oz of Okra
- 2 medium sized Onions
- 1 teaspoon of Sea Salt
- 2 heaped teaspoons of Garam Masala
- 2 heaped teaspoons of Turmeric
- ½ level teaspoon of Chilli powder or 1 small fresh green Chilli finely chopped
- 6 tablespoons of Oil for frying the Okra
- Large frying pan with lid

METHOD:

1. Wash the Okra first and dry really thoroughly with kitchen paper towels, otherwise it will get quite sticky when you get to cook it. Top and tail the Okra and then cut the Okra into thin rounds, about 1cm (approx ½") in size.

2. Cut the Onions into thick odd shaped pieces.

3. Using a large frying pan, heat up the Oil and toss in the Onions, and if using fresh Chillies fry them now with the Onions. Cook until the Onions are golden brown. Add all the spices and the salt next. Fry these for just a few seconds mixing well into the Onions then add the chopped Okra and mix thoroughly. Add 118ml/4fl.oz of cold water and simmer with the frying pan lid on. Cook for 15 to 20 minutes and stir just once or twice, as the Okra is quite delicate and will tend to break up.

Bhindi Sabji is best with Chapatis or Pooris rather than Rice.
I serve it with lots of fresh salad and a dollop of natural soya
or plain Yoghurt on top of the Okra - this makes it look special
and gives the Okra a lovely creamy texture.

CHANNA MASALA

Chick Peas in a rich spicy Tomato sauce in a Sukha stylee!

This is so simple to make and can be eaten with Chapati, Rice, or
even with Chips!

In India, it is eaten as a starter or snack. Serve some of the
Channa Masala over your Samosa, then add some Yoghurt on top
of that - finally garnish it by sprinkling Chat Masala. Yummee!

INGREDIENTS:

- 2 tins /480g of ready boiled Chick Peas. Rinse and drain the
  water out of the tin or soak 240g of dried Chick Peas overnight.
  Then boil them until they are soft.
- Tin of chopped Tomatoes 400g or 4 large Tomatoes
  roughly chopped.
- 3 medium sized Onions – diced
- 3 cloves of Garlic finely chopped
- 2.5cm long and 1cm width (1" long & half an inch wide)
  of Fresh Ginger or 1 level teaspoon of Dried Ginger powder
- ½ level teaspoon of Chilli powder or 1 fresh green Chilli
  very finely chopped
- 2 heaped teaspoons of Garam Masala

3: SABJI

- 2 heaped teaspoons of Turmeric
- 1 level tablespoon of ground Coriander (optional)
- 2 level teaspoons of Salt
- 6 tablespoons of Oil
- 170ml/6fl.oz cold water

METHOD:

Using a big saucepan, fry the Garlic, Onion, Ginger and fresh Chillies until golden brown in the Oil. Add the spices next and mix for just a minute. Add the chopped fresh or tinned Tomatoes and simmer until a thick rich sauce appears. Next add the tinned Chick Peas or your boiled Chick Peas and the cold water, cover and simmer for 5 minutes so that the spices can seep into them.

Serves 4 to 6 people. Garnish it with either Yoghurt and Chat Masala powder, or Black Pepper and Coriander leaves.

 ## DURRI SABJI

These are lighter dishes and the sauce is a rich thin texture. Again you can experiment with various vegetables. I have chosen the following:

3: SABJI

ALOO MUTTER & GAJRA – Potatoes, Peas & Carrots
KHUMBI – Mushroom dish

 ## ALOO MUTTER & GAJRA SABJI – Durri style

Potatoes, Peas and Carrots

INGREDIENTS:

- 3 medium sized Onions finely diced
- 2 medium sized Carrots – finely sliced into rounds
- 2 medium sized Potatoes
- 3 cloves of Garlic very finely chopped
- 2.5cm long, 1cm width of fresh Ginger (or l level teaspoon of Ginger powder)
- 2 heaped teaspoons of Turmeric
- 2 heaped teaspoons of Garam Masala
- ½ level teaspoon of Chilli powder or 1 fresh green Chilli finely chopped
- 2 level teaspoons of Salt
- 250g/9oz of Peas (fresh or frozen). Try using fresh Peas, as they taste simply wonderful in this recipe.
- 3 medium fresh Tomatoes chopped finely or a small tin of tomatoes (225g)
- 1 litre (approximately 2 pints) of boiling water
- 2 tablespoons of Coriander leaves
- 6 tablespoons of oil
- Large pan

3: SABJI

METHOD:

1. Fry the chopped Onion, Ginger and Garlic and fresh Chillies until golden, stirring occasionally.

2. Add the Turmeric, Garam Masala, Salt, and Chilli powder. Stir for half a minute. Add the Tomatoes and reduce the heat to allow all the spices to simmer into the Tomatoes, stirring very occasionally, for about 3 minutes for a rich sauce.

3. Add the Potatoes, Carrots and (only the Fresh Peas now) as they will take as much cooking time as the Potatoes. Mix thoroughly until all the rich spicy tomato sauce covers the Peas, Carrots and Potatoes and add the boiling water. Stir and bring to the boil and then reduce the heat. Put the saucepan lid on. When the Potatoes are soft you know that the dish is done. (If using Frozen Peas, simply add these just before the Potatoes and Carrots are almost cooked).

Before serving add fresh unchopped Coriander leaves. They float on top like beautiful water flowers and gives this dish a sweet fragrance. A lovely summer dish, especially if you use Fresh Peas.

3: SABJI

 KHUMBI SABJI

Durri Mushrooms

This Sabji takes only a very short time to cook. Serve with hot Roti or Poori.

INGREDIENTS:

• 460/16oz Fresh Mushrooms - chop into thick pieces, then use the same ingredients as the Channa Masala dish on Page 30.

METHOD:

1. Once the Onions and Spices and Tomatoes have blended together to make a rich sauce, add the chopped Mushrooms and mix thoroughly.

2. Add 250ml (½ pint) of boiling water and cook for five minutes.

(If you do want the sauce to be watery you can make this dish in a Sukha style too by cooking it with 170ml/6fl.oz of boiling water instead).

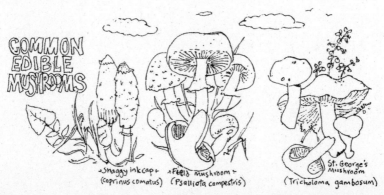

4: DHAL

Dhal made from beans or pulses plays a very important part especially in North Indian cooking, as it is high in protein and fibre and tends to be eaten at most meal times.

The easiest way to make Dhal in my opinion is to boil the pulses/beans first, then add a "Tarka" which means a "garnish". I prefer to use Olive Oil for making Tarka Masala Dhal.

To make TARKA Masala Dhal using Red Lentils, you will need:

INGREDIENTS:

+ 1 packet of Red Lentils 225g/8oz
+ 1 level teaspoon of Cumin seeds (optional)
+ 1 heaped teaspoon of Garam Masala
+ 1 heaped teaspoon of Turmeric
+ 2 cloves of Garlic finely chopped
+ 1 level teaspoon of Salt
+ 1 level teaspoon of Chilli powder or 2 fresh green Chillies finely chopped
+ 2 tablespoons of Olive Oil
+ 1 litre of water

METHOD:

Wash the Lentils with lots of cold water and place the Dhal into a large pan. Add the water and bring to the boil leaving the lid of the pan on at an angle. As it is boiling you will need to remove the white surf that appears. Reduce the heat until the Lentils are soft and it is best to stir the Dhal once or twice, or it may go lumpy.

4: DHAL

It takes about 30 minutes to cook. Leave to one side. Make the
Tarka Masala in a small pan. Heat up the oil, then add the Garlic
and fresh Chilli and fry for one minute until very slightly golden
brown, then add the Cumin seeds and fry for just five seconds as
Cumin seeds are delicate. Next add the Garam Masala, Turmeric,
and Salt, and if not using fresh Chillies, add the Chilli powder
now. Fry for just 20 seconds, as all the spices together burn
very easily. Whilst sizzling hot, pour the Tarka Masala onto the
cooked Lentils and stir.

Use this method and ingredients for any of the pulses you
like and you will certainly transform the texture and enhance
the taste! For a change you could also try adding two large
freshly chopped Tomatoes or half a tin of Tomatoes (200g)
after you have added the spices. This gives the Dhal a thicker,
richer texture.

Tarka Masala Dhal can be made with Red Kidney Beans, Chick
Peas, Black-eyed Beans, Yellow Moong Dhal, or my favourite
Black Moong Urid Linsen. In fact, there are over 60 varieties of
pulses and beans to choose from for North Indian cooking.

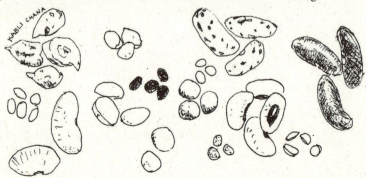

5: RICE

MUTTER CHAWAL

Spicy pilao made with Rice and Peas

I always use Basmati Rice, which by the way is grown in the foothills of the Himalayas. It is a long-shaped delicate grain, which has its own distinctive fragrance. This dish is a childhood favourite of mine; great food for kids to enjoy, and so easy to make.

INGREDIENTS:

+ 225g (8oz) Basmati Rice
+ 1 medium sized Onion cut into small flaky pieces
+ 200g (7oz) Frozen Peas (uncooked)
+ 2 teaspoons Turmeric
+ 2 teaspoons Garam Masala
+ 1 Cinnamon stick, broken into 3 pieces (optional)
+ 1 heaped teaspoon Salt
+ 1 level teaspoons of Cumin Seeds (optional)
+ 6 tablespoon of Sunflower Oil
+ 850ml/1½ pints of hot boiling water

METHOD:

1. Wash the Rice under cold water several times in a large bowl, drain and put to one side.

2. Warm up the oil in a large deep pan and fry the Onion until it is a very light golden brown in colour.

3. Add the Turmeric, Garam Masala, Salt, Cumin and Cinnamon sticks. Fry for just 30 seconds.

Add the Rice next and stir gently to make sure all the spices and onions are mixed into the rice. Finally, add the hot water and stir once more. Bring to the boil and then lower the heat, and keep the lid to the pan on, for 15 minutes.

4. Check the Rice to see if it is cooked by taking a few grains out and tasting it. If cooked, add the Frozen Peas, stirring them into the Rice very carefully. The steam from the Rice will magically cook the frozen Peas!

Mutter Chawal is gorgeous served with fresh Natural Yogurt, or plain Soya Yoghurt, topped with Chat Masala. Serve it as part of your Sabji dishes or just eat it on its own as a snack.

6: RAITA

RAITA

Creamy, chilled spicy yoghurt

I finish with Raita as this usually accompanies all the main
dishes. Raita is a side dish made with chilled Yoghurt - Soya
Yoghurt works really well too and is usually an important part
of every Indian meal. You can experiment using lots of various
spices and ingredients. I tend to keep it simple by using either,
Mint, Cucumber or Coriander. In this recipe I have used
Coriander and Chat Masala powder which creates a delicious
tasty tangy flavour.

INGREDIENTS:

- 250g/9oz tub of PLAIN natural Yoghurt or plain Soya Yoghurt
- 25g/1oz or 1 tablespoon of fresh Coriander leaves also
  finely chopped
- ½ level teaspoon of Salt
- ½ level teaspoon of ground Black Pepper.
- 3 heaped teaspoons of Chat Masala powder
- Half a Cucumber diced with the skin left on

METHOD:

In a large bowl, stir all the spices into the Yoghurt and gently
mix. Taste it to see if it is spicy or salty enough for you -
in fact you won't be able to resist eating the lot! Then add the
diced Cucumber and Coriander leaves and then simply
mix this altogether and the Raita is ready. Keep chilled in the
refrigerator. Serves four people if you have two big dollops each!

Peter Kinnear Burman 1984

❧: NOTES

❧: NOTES

ঔ: NOTES

❧: NOTES